Write Him Off: Journal Prompts to Heal Your Broken Heart in 30 Days

Gratitude Journal: 52 Writing Prompts to Celebrate Your Wonderful Life

The Science of Getting Rich Action Plan: Decoding Wallace D. Wattles's Bestselling Book

7 Days to Minimalistic Living: A Stress-Free Guide to Declutter, Clean and Organize Your Home and Your Life

The Love Book

Writing Your Way to Your Soul Mate

Elizabeth N. Doyd

In practical advice books, like anything else in life, there are no guarantees of results. This book is not intended for use as a source of medical advice. All readers are advised to seek services of competent professionals in the medical field as needed.

ISBN-13: 978-0993949586

ISBN-10: 0993949584

Contents

Introduction

If your soul mate were to knock on your door right now, would you be ready to receive this amazing person into your life?

If you have the desire to be with a soul mate, love is not only possible, it's your destiny. The creator wants to give us all the good things in life. In order to receive them, we need to work to remove the negativity and blockages we have put up ourselves in this lifetime, and in previous lifetimes.

Part One of this book will help you remove any blockages to love with journal writing exercises. You might have to dig up some old pains, fears and insecurities for you to release them. You'll be doing some heavy inner work and it may not be easy, but it's necessary to make the space in your heart to welcome in love.

In Part Two, we'll get to the fun stuff—letting your soul mate in! You'll get to create your dream relationship, make a vision board, learn to keep your love vibration high, and make a bucket list of all the things you want to do with your soul mate once you are together.

You don't have to be perfect to receive love. The key is to be as happy and as grateful as possible. Like attracts like, according to the law of attraction, so what attracts love? Love. As long as you are doing your best to replace old negative patterns with new positive ways of thinking, the universe will conspire for you to meet the right person at the right time. Don't worry if you fall into despair from time to time. Positive feelings and heart energy is stronger than any negative energy you may have, so focus on the good. Just 51% of positive energy is enough, since it's the tipping point for things to go your way.

It's a lot easier to feel love after you've shed light on your deep-rooted thoughts and beliefs and eradicate them. If you believe that you are not worthy of love, then guess what? You'll manifest the reality. But if you maintain self-love and faith, you'll attract your soul mate faster.

I'm giving you all the knowledge I've acquired in the field of love and relationships from my twenty years of spiritual studies and in my eleven years of being a relationship expert, where I've helped my local clients do what you're about to do: make some big inner shifts and attract soul mate love.

You don't have to hit the bars and pretend to be someone you're not with this work, but you do have to go out of your comfort zone in other ways.

This book contains plenty of journal writing exercises because journaling is an effective technique used by psychologists, psychiatrists and other coaches. When we lay down our deepest, toughest feelings in writing, we can examine our internal mechanisms so that we can make the necessary changes in our daily lives.

Try to do the exercises every day. Some chapters contain exercises that may require more than one day to do them, so if you need the extra time, that's okay.

Buy a notebook just for this topic. Name it "The Love Book", "My Soul Mate Journal", or the like. If you resist doing any of the exercises, ask yourself why. Could this be another blockage to love?

After you've done this powerful work, you won't be projecting your insecurities, fears and other personal issues onto your partner. You won't make your soul mate the sole purpose of existence.

This book is not just about how to find someone to be with. It's also about discovering yourself, what you really want, and uncovering your true purpose in life. When you're whole and complete, you won't exude the energy of neediness and desperation that is so counterproductive in attracting love.

The fact that you've bought this book tells me that you are ready to go on this journey and receive the love you deserve. I believe that everyone already has all the answers within themselves. You only need to tap into it. Listen to your higher self. Write it out. My job is guide you along the way.

I hope the lessons resonate with you. You have nothing to lose by doing these exercises. Love might come sooner than you think, but remember to enjoy every moment of your journey along the way.

—Elizabeth N. Doyd

What is the purpose of romantic love?

There are many roads to love. For some, there's instant attraction, love at first sight striking a thunderbolt into their hearts. Other times, two people meet and they're totally repelled by each other at first, until they get to know each other better. Some may start out as friends, thinking they have no romantic chemistry, but gradually develop a deep and faithful love. So love has all sorts of beginnings, but how can you ensure that your relationship lasts a lifetime?

First, you must understand the purpose of romantic love, and love in general. We each come into this world yearning for our other half. It's our destiny. We also need to understand that all souls come from One: we are all one soul, so in a way, we are all soul mates. We can have soul mate relationships with our siblings, our bosses and our friends.

Soul mate relationships can be developed when both parties make the effort.

Life is all about relationships. They're as challenging as they are fulfilling. Other people reflect the good in us and the garbage in us. They support us while showing us our blind spots, clarifying what what we need to work on to be better people.

Romantic relationships do this on a deeper level, which is why it can give us as much heartache as it can the most elevated bliss on earth. If monogamy scares you, you're really scared of true intimacy, the heart to heart worship. Are you afraid of someone seeing you—all of you—completely?

Relationships give us the opportunity to fill our souls with lasting joy. There are people who can make us temporarily happy and there are people who can bring us unending happiness for all eternity, and vice versa. If we are not as happy as we want to be, it is because we haven't found the right people in our lives yet, socially, romantically or in business.

How do we draw the right people into our lives? By connecting to the Divine Light, God, a higher power, a higher source, positive energy, or whatever you want to call it.

While people are the key to our joy, they are not the cause and we the effect. God, on the other hand, is the cause of all causes. Inspiration, creative thought, premonition and intuition come from this place. God's love is always in us and around us, and we must make a connection within. The love we seek is already available to us.

When we seek heaven in the external, it's nowhere to be found. We think we love others, but it's actually need. There's a big difference. What did you like about your last relationship? "They make me feel loved. They understand me. They make me feel secure." These are typical responses. All relationships start out as a form of need, however. We are always seeking to fulfill our own desires by default.

It's only through spiritual growth that we learn to love the other person unconditionally, to love in order to see the other person happy without expecting anything from them in return.

When this happens, the pleasure we derive is from pleasing and fulfilling the other. Our partner would feel the same about us.

We receive because we know that receiving our partner's love gives them happiness. A wonderful circuitry of love is then established, where the act of receiving is transformed into the act of sharing. This powerful dynamic creates miracles and divine pleasure for those involved. To get to this place, we must work on personal transformation.

Loving another helps the soul evolve. That's why the initial connection with the Divine is so important. If you trust God to know your heart and to deliver the right person into your life, you are not out there looking for the wrong person and reacting to the fear of being alone.

You will come together with a partner who shares the same goals and values, the same desires to please one another. As we know by now, like attracts like, but this doesn't mean attracting someone exactly like you. You'll attract someone with the same morals and ethics, but with complementary traits and talents. For example, one person can be creative and the other person can be business-minded, while still having the common end goal of bringing more love into the world.

You might have felt that you've had deep connections in the past with other partners. Yes, you can even call them soul mate relationships, since we are all soul mates. But just because you were together and had a powerful bond doesn't mean the relationship was meant to last a lifetime. You might have had soul contracts drawn up and needed to come together to work on your karma, or to heal so you can open up to your true love.

Learn from the past and let it go. If they were meant to be in your life, it would've happened, so be open and never settle. Listen to you intuition and not your immediate needs (for intimacy, love, security, etc).

Sometimes we're convinced that someone is our soul mate, when they could've been someone we've known from a past life. The strong sense of familiarity with the person can make us think they're the right one, when they might not be the best fit.

Romantic love can fun, romantic and full of hot, intense chemistry. But unlike the movies where the story ends with a wedding, there's more to the tale.

In a relationship, there's work to be done to correct our souls. Both partners must work to let go of their negative traits. In a romantic relationship, our garbage becomes much clearer, because we're letting someone in on a deeper level. Scary? Maybe. But it's absolutely transformational for our souls and completely rewarding. Both partners must share their positive traits and opinions with each other so both views can be embraced.

It's all about being open, sharing, caring, and learning to remove judgment, fear, anger and other negativity. Like with any relationships, even the most peaceful ones, the road might get bumpy sometimes, and there will be stress, but there will also be a foundation of respect, dignity and deep love to strength the relationship as you grow together.

Some people resist love because they want to avoid this type of deep transformation. But when a true soul connection takes place, it's awe-inspiring. The other person becomes a recipient for sharing, for what we have to offer. There's great friendship, a comfortable ease in our interactions, an unspoken emotional connection, as well as crazy chemistry.

How do we receive this type of love? First, we must decide that we want it.

PART ONE: Getting Ready

ONE
Set Your Intention

Why do you want love? Take a few minutes to list all the reasons why you want a partner in your life.

If you were in a loving relationship, how would your life be different?

Get clear: do you want to be in a long-term relationship? If so, does that mean marriage? Do you want kids?

State your relationship intention by finishing this sentence:

"By doing all the exercises in my Love Book, I intend to manifest…"

TWO
How Do You Believe?

Do you truly, deeply believe that your desire for big love can be realized? Explore why or why not.

If you don't believe you'll ever find your soulmate, or that s/he doesn't exist, then does it really surprise you when you get to be right? If you believe that your soul mate is not only out there, but also looking for you too, you open the door for true love to enter.

Maybe you're conflicted. A part of you tells yourself that love is not in the cards for you, but another part knows that you want love more than anything and that it can happen for you. Which voice do you listen to?

Don't worry. You're not alone. Many people have false beliefs swirling around in their heads. If everyone had certainty that they could have love, they would walking hand in hand with their soul mates. You can get there. You're reading this book and already taking action by doing the exercises, preparing yourself for big love to come in. Your job right now is to do your best to dispel all the negative beliefs, thought patterns, fears and doubts that have been blocking you from letting love in.

Close your eyes. Can you imagine yourself in a loving relationship? Can you imagine being so in love with someone and having this special person equally love you back? Can you see yourself cherished for not just your good traits, but warts and all? Write in your journal why or why not.

Be honest. You're beginning to uncover your subconscious beliefs that have been keeping you stuck. The reason why this is so important is because what you believe on the subconscious level about yourself is continually communicated to others.

For example, if you believe deep down that you are unlovable, you can do and say all the right things, but you are still able to subconsciously "talk" the person you are dating out of loving you. Sometimes relationships don't last because after the initial passion wears off, our deep insecurities and fears become more apparent to each other. Your partner wants to compliment you, not reassure you. If you are depending on someone to validate your self-worth, it's not going to work and they will get tired of doing so in the long run.

Ask yourself where these limiting beliefs are coming from. It could've been an idea that had been instilled in you growing up. Intense emotional events (such as verbal abuse, sexual abuse, etc.) could have triggered feelings of shame, guilt and unworthiness. When you were young, the criticisms from authority figures such as parents and teachers might have been taken seriously. Your peers, the society and your environment can also have a huge impact on what you believe to be true, such as how hard it is to find love, or that you're nothing if you're single. The subconscious mind can either accept or reject an idea to be true. The universe, your reality, is like a mirror that reflects your beliefs.

Even if you've carried some deep-rooted beliefs about yourself, you can still turn them around. You don't need to be perfect to find love. Our souls are already perfect. You just need to work on yourself enough that 51% of your beliefs about love and about yourself are positive ones. 51% is the tipping point. So don't worry if you still have some lingering negative feelings and doubts by the end of this program. As long as you try, the universe will support your journey to true love and long-lasting fulfillment.

THREE
Season of Singleness

How do you feel about being single? Write it all down. What's painful about it? What good has it done for you and your life? Is singleness a sentence? Or is it an opportunity?

For those who are not enjoying their season of singleness, know this:

During your single years, you can either find yourself or lose yourself. This is a time to really get to know yourself, what your purpose is, what you love to do, what you want and don't want in a relationship, and much more. If you allow your fears and desperation to dictate your choice in a mate, you'll lower your standards and tolerate anything in a relationship. When you lack your own dreams and identity, you'll latch on to your partner's dreams and find your identity in another person.

If your main concern is to be accepted and wanted by someone, you won't be able to stand on your own two feet because you'll be clinging to someone else in order to be secure and happy. When you're seeking external reassurance and making someone else the source of your livelihood, your long-term goals and personal dreams may fade or even disappear altogether.

To be blunt: get over it. The last thing anyone needs is a partner who is needy, desperate and insecure. Would you want to date someone this codependent? Probably not. And anyone who does probably prefers to feel superior to their partner. They might have a thirst for dominance and might have the same fears and insecurities.

If you've been depressed by all the bad dates you've been on, you could probably benefit from a dating detox. This can last anywhere from two weeks to 90 days. If you just got out of a long-term relationship, the detox can be on the longer end of the spectrum. Be careful not to let this period last too long since you might end up enjoying it too much!

During this time, stop looking for dates and stop dating. This is a time to get to know yourself. **What do you like doing?** Is it reading, going to the movies, walking your dog, volunteering, cooking, fishing, catching up with friends, or even traveling somewhere exotic?

What makes you feel good? Do you like massages, laughing, taking long bubble baths, listening to music, doing yoga, dancing, taking walks in the park? The point is, this time is all about YOU. Get in touch with yourself again. Find all the ways to make yourself happy and balanced.

There's a lot to enjoy when you're single that you will probably miss once you are in a couple. **Make a list of them!** For example, you can the bed and the blanket, eat whatever you want, your schedule is more flexible, and you don't need to get permission to do anything or to check in with anyone. You get to spend all the money you make on yourself. You get to put yourself first.

This is not to say there is something wrong with the desire to be with another person. God put that desire in us for a reason: we are meant to share love with a romantic partner. However, if you're single, embrace the present. It's only one snapshot of your life that can change in an instant, so enjoy it while you can. Many people who are now married with children wonder why they spent so many years miserable when they had the freedom and time to have fun. Your love is on the way; you just haven't met this person yet, so in the meantime, do the things you really want to do. I can't stress this enough.

You can spend your single time resenting happy couples or you can spend this time developing yourself, becoming a stronger, more secure, and happier person.

You might be single in order to learn something that you can't when you're in a couple. Maybe you need to work out your kinks so that you'll attract someone dynamite. Many of the things you're learning now can prepare you for a great marriage. The stronger your sense of self, the happier you'll be in a relationship.

It might feel like you're taking the long road when everybody else has a secret shortcut, but you're not.

The creator always gives you what you need. Being in a relationship doesn't mean you'll be on cloud nine all the time.

When others rush to get married, they might not have the wisdom of knowing who they are outside of their marriage, because they haven't given themselves the chance to explore that. The divorce rate is so high partly because people marry without taking the time to find out if they are truly compatible.

Take the time to get to know yourself. Take the time to get to know a potential partner. Wait for the right relationship to come in that will last. If you try to fill the void meant for your soulmate with a mediocre relationship, you're rejecting the possibility of the right thing. Wait for the right thing.

If you're single because you're afraid of love, you have to make a decision. **Is love even worth the risk?** Abuse, infidelity and drama are associated with love, but they are not love. **Decide that you want love more than you are afraid of it.**

FOUR
Release Your Negative Beliefs About Love

I've met a few men and women who'd settled in their romantic lives out of fear, as well as people who chose to remain single, insisting that life is easier when they're alone. That's their choice.

It's all about desire. If you can be open and acknowledge that, yes, deep down, true love is what you really want, it can be yours. If you want to be happily married, how can you be if you have a full list arguing *against* marriage?

What are your fears and negative beliefs about love? These are just some common examples:

"There are no good men/women left."
"I'm too old/fat/ugly to get love."
"Everybody gets love except me."

"Love will get in the way of my work and independence."
"I'll only get cheated on if I let love in."

Write down every single fear you have. List all the cynical remarks you've ever made about the opposite sex and dating. Write down everything that has ever wounded your heart so far in life. Be thorough.

Leave 2 to 3 lines blank under each statement.

If it helps to get out every single bad belief, finish these sentences:

"The reason I can't have my soul mate is because…"
"When I think of marriage, I think of…"
"I'm single because…"

Do any of your negative responses ring true?

Now we're going to go back and **turn each negative belief into a positive statement.** Cross out the negative one, then write the positive statement underneath. Use a different colored pen for the positive statements, preferably red, as it's believed to have activating energy.

For example, *"I'll only get cheated on if I let love in,"* can be crossed out and followed with, *"My partner is faithful and s/he truly loves and cherishes me."*

Do this for every statement.

To let go of your negative beliefs further, copy the negative lines onto a loose page. Turn this into a releasing ritual by burning this page. As you watch the paper burn, feel your old negative patterns of thinking dissolve. Say aloud, "I release all my negative beliefs about love and all of my past pain. This is all behind me now."

Look at the positive statements in red in your journal. Say aloud, *"I now accept these new positive beliefs to replace my old negative patterns."* Read each line and feel the love coming from each statement. Say, *"My amazing love life starts now."* Feel it in your heart.

Another way to release old negative thoughts is by examining it when it comes. Ask yourself, "does this thought or pain belong to me?" It could be someone else's fears, such as a friend's or your mother's, or our society's collective consciousness. If it's not your thought, say aloud, "return to sender." You might feel an immediate weight lifted off your chest. By sending the thought back, you're helping break the chain of negativity.

Negative influence will try its best to make a comeback in your thoughts—after all, they've made a home in your head for so many years. When it comes, continue to examine it and question its validity. Chances are, it'll dissipate. If you're really having a hard time letting go of certain thoughts, I recommend a method by Bryon Katie called "The Work". It consists of 4 main questions to ask yourself. You can learn more about "The Work" and download the worksheets for free on her website at: www.thework.com/thework-4questions.php

FIVE
Release Your Negative Beliefs About Yourself

Look at yourself in the mirror. Which features do you like? Which ones do you avoid looking at?

Write down what you like and don't like about your appearance.

Are there certain things on the list you can control? If you are feeling frumpy in outdated clothes, figure out what kind of clothes you do want to incorporate into your wardrobe by looking at magazines or asking a fashionable friend for advice. Go out and buy clothes you can feel good in. While wearing sweats and sneakers won't keep your soulmate from you, if you feel good in beautiful, well-made clothes, why not dress this way often? You really do walk and carry yourself differently in nice clothes.

If you hate your haircut, go to the hair salon. If you want to get fit, go to the gym and make a plan to eat healthier. There's nothing wrong in wanting to look your best. If you at least keep up with basic grooming, you're doing everyone around you a favor. You deserve the best and to feel the best. A beautiful soul should be kept in a beautiful shell. You wouldn't keep fresh flowers in a torn up cardboard box, would you?

That said, you don't need to look perfect and flawless like an airbrushed magazine model to be with your soulmate. If you don't change a thing about yourself, you can still be with your soulmate, but if you don't believe that you are in your best physical state to be in a relationship, what's blocking love from you is this belief.

If you go outside right now, you'll see dozens of people in relationships who exhibit the same qualities in yourself that you don't find attractive. Love found them and it can be yours too.

The goal is to feel healthy, happy and confident.

What traits do you hide from your dates? It could be a physical trait or a personality trait. If you're unsure, look at what you judge harshly in others.

Now think about past lovers, friends and family members for whom this trait is not a big deal. They love you anyway. Write about this, then follow it with, *"I forgive myself for judging myself to be...."*

Close your eyes and visualize your soulmate discovering your flaw, and not only loving you anyway, but telling you that it's endearing and amusing. **Describe this revelation and how it makes you feel.**

What other negative thoughts do you have about yourself? Do you believe you're dumb? Unsuccessful? Too shy? Boring? Turn them around by changing the perspective and reframing them into positive statements. Use a red pen for the positive statements.

"I'm ugly," turns into *"I am beautiful. I'm radiant in the eyes of God. My soulmate can't get enough of me."*

"I'm stupid," turns into *"I'm wise. Just because I made a mistake doesn't mean I am worthless. Everyone makes mistakes."*

"He doesn't notice me," turns into *"The right person will see me. My soulmate will be drawn to me and won't hesitate to talk to me."*

And so on. When you catch yourself putting yourself down, catch yourself and correct it by giving it a new, positive perspective.

Remember that there's no such thing as rejection. Other people's judgements reflect on themselves and their own insecurities. In fact, they must've been feeling pretty horrible to have lashed out on you. While this doesn't excuse their behavior, know that this is not an accurate reflection on you and your worth.

It's important to learn this because when you have insecurities and feelings of unworthiness, you will look for reassurance in your partner, and this is unhealthy. This is why you must elevate your confidence. This means not settling for less than what you want. **Set your intention to stop destructive behaviors that get in the way of love.**

Some examples:

"I'm letting go of men/women who won't commit."
"I'm willing to stop using sex/my sexuality to get love and intimacy."
"I'm willing to let go of married men."
"I'm willing to stop bending over backwards to convince someone to love me."

When you're done, write and say aloud: *"I release my past and I am free. All of my negative attitudes are now gone. I love and appreciate myself!"*

SIX
Declutter Your Heart

To make room for the new, it makes sense to get rid of the old. If there are any past lovers who still have energetic hooks in you, sever those ties. Ideally you should be completely released from your ex, but even if you have a little opening for your soulmate to come in, it's enough.

Before you do a release, let's figure out what we have to learn from your exes. Draw a line down the middle of a page. Write "Positive Traits" on one side and "Negative Traits" on the other. Think of each ex and write under the appropriate columns the positive qualities that attracted you to them, and the negative things you didn't like. Do you see a pattern in either column?

You may be wondering why your past relationships haven't worked out. You might've had to come together to work out any karma you had together. In Kabbalah, it is said that you attract those you've known in previous lives, which is why you feel a certain jolt of emotion when you meet certain strangers. Your ex might've reflected your childhood woulds, which enabled you to release them. Even if the relationship was a rocky one, it could've helped you heal in an aspect of your life that needed healing or closure. You might've had to come together to do some special work, or have children together. When your work was completed, you might've grown apart and wanted different things. Some relationships do have expiration dates.

Your past relationships teach you lessons and prepare you for your soulmate, the person you'll have lasting fulfillment and joy with. It's something to be grateful for.

By letting go of your exes, you'll stop wasting your time and energy on unrequited love. It'll make you wide open to your soulmate. Release the anger and bitterness you're harboring over past relationships so your heart is light.

If your ex is still in your life and you still have feelings for this person, create distance between the two of you for a while. Don't talk yourself into thinking that being friends, or friends with benefits, is a good idea. That's just giving yourself false hope. We all tend to think our last love was the love of our life, but sometimes when you get over your ex, you'll ask yourself, "What was I thinking?"

Forgive yourself if you've made some bad choices for partners. No matter how smart you are, you might still make terrible choices. Don't berate yourself. Even Elizabeth Bennett fell for the conniving Wickham and wrote Darcy off before she finally came to her senses!

The past has taught you something, and you're ready to move on. Make your mind up that you are ready to release. **Make a list of ex-lovers whom you still haven't gotten over. Write a letter to each of them expressing in detail the reasons why you are still angry and things you wish had turned out differently.** You're not going to mail these letters, so let yourself write whatever that comes to mind. Acknowledge your role in the demise of the relationship and apologize for anything you've done that you regret.

Write a second letter from their perspective, to you. It's easier to do this than you think. Imagine them sitting in front of you. See what they saw and feel what they felt.

When you're finished writing, close your eyes and imagine a cord between the two of you. Cut this cord and see him/her flying away. Say aloud, "I release you to your highest good."

Wish them the best. It's okay to still have love and

goodwill for your ex. Love is always inside you. When a relationship no longer serves you, you can love from a distance without being attached. Every time you get sad about the demise of this relationship, repeat, "I release you to your highest good." Turn your focus to how much joy you'll feel when you are in the arms of your new love, the soulmate you feel right at home with.

Congratulation yourself for making any headway. Some people hold on and never learn to let go. Doing this is big for self-growth.

The exercises here may be enough for some people. If you need to go further, I have another book called *Write Him Off: Journal Prompts to Heal Your Broken Heart in 30 Days* that will help you let go on a deeper level.

SEVEN
Parental Love

Not only did our parents pass down their genes to us, they were our first role models for romantic relationships. It's worth examining what we've learned from them, consciously or subconsciously.

Write "Father" on top of one page. Draw a line down the middle of the page. Write "Positive Traits" above one column and "Negative Traits" in the other.

Make another page for your mother.

List what you like about each parent and what you don't like.

On a third page, write "Marriage" on top of the page and draw a line down the middle of the page again. Write "Good" on one column and "Bad" on the other. **List the good and bad things you learned about marriage/romantic relationships** from your parents as a child.

On a fourth page, make another "Good/Bad" page, with the heading "My Last 3 Relationships". **Write what you liked and didn't like about your last three relationships.**

Now make a page for "Me". **What do you like or dislike about yourself as an adult?**

What kind of conclusions can you draw from these pages? Does any of the traits from your mother's or father's pages correspond with the traits of your exes?

Do your past relationship(s) have commonalities with your parents' marriage?

Do you share similar traits with your parents?

EIGHT
Forgiving Others

Sometimes we harbor deep-rooted pain or resentment towards certain people in our lives. It could be a parent who was critical, abusive, overbearing, or simply unavailable. It could be a classmate who bullied you. It could be an ex who made you feel worthless. It could be a teacher who made you feel stupid in class.

We might tell ourselves that what they've said or done doesn't affect us anymore, but there might still be some pain lingering. You're hurt that your mother never told you she loved you. You're hurt that bullies teased you about your weight. You're hurt that an ex-boyfriend cheated on you. You're hurt that a teacher told you you'd never amount to anything.

Many of these things might have happened in your childhood. You're an adult now. While you should reclaim who you are as a man or a woman, do take care of your inner child. Give him or her a hug. Tell your younger self that you are loved and you are perfect no matter what.

You can start to heal from past hurts by listing every person who has ever wronged you. The reason for this exercise is to get rid of those resentments the best you can, and heal those emotional needs so you don't project the anger and hurt onto a future partner.

Stop burying the pain because they're still going to be there, and they might even erupt unexpectedly. They may even be the cause of emotional eating, self-mutilation, promiscuity, addictions, and other such behaviors. When you feel you are deprived of love, you might look for it in other places. It may also affect your love life because you may be afraid of rejection and criticism, and subconsciously push others away.

Use a page for each person you're angry with. Write about what they've done and how their actions have affected your life. Explore why they would want you to experience this trauma. Why would they want this outcome for you? Are they really evil, or do they have their own reason to cause harm, such as their own history of abuse, trauma, mental illness, addictions, and other situations?

If you're angry with your parents, more often than

not, the problem is generational. If your father had trouble expressing love for you, one of his parents might have done the same to him and so on. You can break the chain and stop this way of behaving by acknowledging this, healing and moving on.

If one of your parents abandoned you, have you considered that maybe they didn't feel worthy to be your parent? They might have had some emotional issues they couldn't handle, and didn't think they would be a positive influence in your life.

If your teacher or your peer made you feel bad about yourself, do you think they were happy with themselves?

Now explore how you would feel if you didn't carry this resentment anymore.

At the end of each letter, write and say aloud, "I understand now that you did this because (cause of their action) and not because you wanted to".

Close your eyes and visualize this person as a scared child. Feel their pain and how bad they must've felt to abuse and harm others. Send the person love and compassion. Let him or her know that you forgive them and hope that they heal.

Imagine a dark box inside you that holds all of your anger toward this person. This is your emotional block that keeps you stuck. See the box come out of your body and dissolve. As you watch it go, feel your resentment, anger and other negative emotions disappear as well. If it feels right, imagine a golden cord connecting you with this person, signifying a healthy relationship.

How do you feel after doing this?

If you are feeling any resistance to do this exercise, ask yourself what is the benefit of holding on to the resentment towards (person)? Letting go and forgiving them doesn't excuse their responsibility from their own actions, but forgiveness gives YOU freedom. You're telling the universe that you won't allow your past to control your life. Your subconscious mind doesn't know the difference between what you wish on others and what you wish for yourself, so it's in your best interest to let go of any anger and ill will towards others.

NINE
Forgiving Yourself

Continuing on with the forgiveness work, sometimes the person we most have to forgive is ourself. What did you do to make yourself feel that you don't deserve love?

Write down what you did and how old you were. How did your action(s) affect you? Why do you think you did that? Do you really believe you meant to hurt yourself or others? How would your life be different if you didn't have this regret or resentment toward yourself?

Close your eyes and imagine yourself in front of you at the age when the incident happened. Tell this younger self what you did and how your actions affected you. Then write and say aloud, *"I understand now why you did what you did because (reason for action) and not because you wanted me to (result of action)."*

See yourself as naive and innocent, feel how you

had felt back then. Send your younger self love and compassion, letting them know you wish them healing and forgiveness. Imagine a white light surrounding your younger self, filling him/her with all the wisdom you've gained over the years. Watch your younger self grow up before your eyes, whole and healed. Any regrets, anger, resentment and other negative emotions become black smoke rising out of you and disappearing into the air. See your younger self and the present-day you merge as one. You are healed and the past is forgiven. You can

now move forward in peace.

TEN
The Greatness in You

Look in the mirror and say to yourself, *"I love you. You are beautiful."*

How do you feel?

What about:

You are talented.
You are intelligent.
You are successful.
You are creative.
You are sexy.
You are happy.
You have a lot to offer.
You love the world and the world loves you.

Do any of these statements make you feel uncomfortable? Did you feel an urge to resist taking the compliment?

Denying your own greatness is something you need to get over. It's true: you're amazing. Pump yourself up. Don't worry about being arrogant. Arrogance is a form of insecurity. True confidence and self-love also makes other people feel good. It's positive and infectious, a powerful magnet.

Start by listing all the great things you have to offer. Whether it's your humor, your passion, your smile and other physical traits, write down every little thing. List all your accomplishments from childhood to present day.

If you want to go further, choose 3 people you're close to. **Write 3 or more personality traits they like about you.** What about your coworkers? How do you excel at your work?

Now imagine God watching you with loving eyes. **If God could name your top 3 qualities, what would they be?**

Still have that voice telling you you're not good enough? In what ways do you believe you are lacking? Every child is born whole and perfect. As we grow up, messages from advertising and the people around us seep into our minds on a subconscious level; judgments from parents, teachers and friends are internalized, making us believe that we are flawed. It's all false.

You don't have to change a thing about yourself to get love right now.

Now imagine your soul mate loving you. What does s/he love about you?

ELEVEN
The Giver

Do you find it hard to say no? Do you give too much, to the point of being a doormat? Do you tend to rescue people? Does all the giving and rescuing drain you of energy a lot of the time?

While generosity is a positive trait, many people, particularly women, tend to over-give. When this happens, this positive trait becomes a weakness. You're not truly giving if you do so in order for people to like you. Nor is it good for your self-esteem when you over-give to make up for something you believe you lack.

Take a look at the list you made of how great you are. How many of those are giver/rescuer traits? Do your friends and family like you for the things you do for them?

If you tend to rescue people, are you rescuing others to avoid your own problems? If so, what are you avoiding? Sometimes this is learnt behavior. Maybe we've witnessed a family member who was always rescuing others, and we've internalized that we need to save others in order to be worthy of love.

It's not unusual for givers to have a hard time receiving love and help from other people.

Do you accept love freely, or do you feel guilty or undeserving, as if you are in debt to the giver when you do receive?

If you've identified yourself as a giver, take a look at the people benefiting around you. Are your friends purely takers? It can be draining when a relationship is one sided. Both sides need to be able to give and receive. To learn this will serve you well in a romantic relationship.

Have you been taken advantage of in the past for your generosity? When you gave, was it genuine?

When you are confident knowing that you don't need to bend over backwards to make the other person stay, you'll attract people who will appreciate you for you, and not what you can do for them.

If you are in a relationship where you are doing most of the giving, try to change it. Ask a favor from your friend and see how s/he responds. If your friend doesn't want to listen to you or support you, the friendship is not serving you. Release this person, or at least put some distance between you, especially if they are family. Since they were used to the dynamic of the relationship, they might need to be eased into this new dynamic of equal give and take.

If it comes to it, you might have to make your boundaries clear and be direct in a kind way. It may be stressful for those who do not like confrontation, but this is terrific for self-growth. Stand up for yourself. Honor yourself. If the people around you don't honor you or your time, it's time to evaluate whether they need to be in your life. If you are really stressed by confrontation, you can gradually drift apart from them.

Tell yourself:

I am whole and complete.
I give to myself first and then I can give to others.
I am responsible only for myself.
I give and receive love freely.

Sometimes the best way to give to a person is by saying "No". This way, you're giving this person the opportunity to help themselves, to be more independent, or to see how their behavior affects others so they can change it. When you give too much, people take for granted what comes easily. They value what they earn, so give to them by giving them an opportunity to earn.

On top of learning how to say no, you can also learn to receive by accepting help from others. Let people do things for you. Ask for help. Accept it graciously when it comes and give the proper thanks.

TWELVE
The Receiver

If I tell you that your soul mate is about to knock on your door right now, how ready are you to receive this person? S/he is smart, funny, talented and loving. This person knows how to have fun and s/he is gorgeous and successful, everything you ever wanted and more. Will you receive this person with open arms, or will you freak out and panic? Write your response in detail in your journal. This will gauge how ready you are for love.

Do you have an "I don't need a man/woman to be happy" attitude when you are secretly craving a relationship?

Are you too busy with work or school?

Do you have a big project that's taking up all your time, and you believe that you'll only have time for love when it's completed?

Do you have big responsibilities like taking care of

a sick parent or being a single mom to three kids?

Know that nothing will get in your way of love. Love can happen anytime, anywhere. You just need to change your way of thinking and to make room in your life for love.

There's an independence trap that some people fall into. They find it easier not to rely on anyone and withdraw from love. But love comes in through vulnerability. If you have been career-focused with a major wall up in the love department, try to have at least a small opening for love prospects to come in. If you don't even have time for yourself, make a plan to pare down your work hours so your life doesn't surround your job and achievements all the time.

We are all interdependent people with the need for love, contact and connection. Otherwise, we'd be hermits in the middle of the mountain somewhere. Being emotionally open doesn't make a person weak. It's a powerful quality, because a person like this doesn't let rejection get in the way of getting what they want or need.

What kind of obligations do you believe are getting in the way of love for you? List them all down. See if any of them are valid. If so, make a plan to complete this project. If they are not valid, give the belief a positive turnaround statement in red ink.

For example, "I won't have time for love until I finish writing this novel," becomes, "I have time for love. Life never gets in the way of love. My soul mate gives me the freedom to complete my (project) and even contributes great ideas."

"I can't be in love as long as I'm taking care of my sick mom in the hospital," becomes, "My true love supports me during this difficult time and inspires more strength in me. My mom is happy that I have someone who adores me."

THIRTEEN
The Love Delusion

Have you ever clung on to a relationship despite a nagging inner voice telling you that your partner was not the right person for you? **Describe this relationship, the highs and lows, and what your inner voice was trying to communicate to you.**

Society has made us buy into the idea of a certain kind of romantic love that is perpetuated by literature and Hollywood: love stories about affairs, class differences, early death—doomed love affairs full of drama, heartache and suffering. We've come to believe that real-life relationships should also be full of such drama. This is not real love. If you've clung on to this kind of romantic relationship, you weren't in love, you were really addicted to suffering.

High passion and instant chemistry can be fun, but as we all know, lust doesn't sustain a relationship. For a relationship to work long-term, there needs to be more than a shallow connection. Some people resist deep connections by playing the field. Play-boys for example can have unrealistic expectations of women and will dump someone as soon as they become too real, too human. Women can also do this by having "fun" by moving on to the next guy as soon as the passion and whirlwind romance of the initial stages of a relationship settles down. All this prevents them from being truly open and intimate on a deeper level with another person.

Have you ever resisted a deep connection? Write about it in your journal.

So how can we start opening to someone on a deeper level? First, we must connect to our higher purpose. It may sound cliche, but we must love ourselves before someone else can love us. This can be difficult since we have a backward way of approaching love—we demand proof from the outside world first to show us that we are lovable. While love and acceptance is a need for everybody, seeking approval and praise is a never-ending quest. Demanding love from other people always leave us unsatisfied and wanting more.

In order to have empowered relationships, we must tap into the source of love inside ourselves. Love is not external. You ex can't just pour love into you, as if they are saving you from the pain and loneliness of singledom. When you are able to access true love within, you will consistently attract love in the external world. You'll uplift yourself. We'll get to this work more in the coming chapters.

FOURTEEN
Emotional Needs

Why do you really want a partner?

Your deepest desire will drive your destiny, so if you have a need to be loved, your energy holds *need*, not *being loved*. Do you see the difference? The energy you are sending out to the universe is *need*, not *love*. Your core belief is that you are not loved, and you set off to manifest this reality. In order to manifest true love and not the need for love, you must fulfill this unmet need first, then your deepest desire (and the energy you emulate) becomes "feeling loved".

To learn what your emotional needs are, fill in the blank.

"If my deepest desire is to feel_____, what would my soul-mate do to fulfill that?"

If you've answered "loved" (to continue with the

example), **list how you can obtain this feeling on your own.** How would you make yourself feel more loved? Select the things you can do now without a partner to experience the feeling of love. For example, you can write love notes and emails to yourself, you can buy yourself flowers, you can feel more love volunteering at an animal shelter, or do nice things for the people you already love, and so on.

If you're having a hard time coming up with your emotional needs, think of the reasons why you miss your ex. Do you miss having someone who listens to you? Someone to go to the movies with? Someone who appreciates you? Do you like feeling connected? Accepted?

You can also go back and read the response you gave for the question "Why do you want love?" from the first chapter for ideas.

Again, happiness is not external. Whatever love and joy you are feeling is in you. It belongs to you. If you expect another person to deliver happiness to you in a gift box, you're giving up control of your own happiness. If you want love so you don't have to be alone, your deep desire is "not be alone". You'll need someone to fix the ache of loneliness. The goal then is not to be in love, but to avoid loneliness, and who you attract might not be right for you on other levels. But at least you're not alone, right?

If you long to get married, do you want to walk down the aisle so that you can impress others with your catch? For your mother's approval? Financial stability? Being with someone based on false desires will leave you unsatisfied and wanting more.

Fulfilling your emotional needs helps you become more desirable. Your soulmate is not responsible for satisfying your emotional needs. This is someone you can share the love you already have within yourself. If you find out the emotional needs behind each desire, you can do something about false desires so it doesn't pollute your romantic relationship.

It might sound backwards, but you must find ways to be happy without a partner so you can hold the feeling of love. When you do, the law of attraction can't fail. Like attracts like and love will be magnetized to you.

FIFTEEN
Your Living Space

If your soulmate came into your house, would you be proud to give him or her a tour?

If you feel your place is not ready, **make a plan to clean it**. Soap doesn't cost very much. Make your home welcoming, a comfortable love den. If it's full of stuff, declutter. The simple act of getting rid of clutter will welcome in new things, people and situations into your life. Nature hates a vacuum. The faster we clear out the old, the faster we'll draw in the new. Clean our your drawers and start with a clean state! You want to create the physical, emotional and psychological inner space to welcome his or her impending arrival.

Keep up on your errands. If you have a lot of bills to pay for example, take care of it sooner rather than later. Once your soulmate sweeps you off your feet, you may not get down from cloud nine to do your daily tasks.

Make a list of the things you want to complete before your soulmate arrives and the plan to go about doing them.

Maybe you want to stock up on candles to make your place more romantic, or buy new bed sheets. Red or pink bed sheets are supposed to activate love energy, according to the Black Hat style of Feng Shui. If you sleep on a bed you've shared with your ex, get a new mattress or a new bed all together. It that's not within your means, new bed sheets will do.

Make space in your home for your soulmate. If you've taken up the whole bed until now, sleep on one side. Clear out the side table on your soulmate's side. You might even want to buy extra towels or pyjamas for your beloved.

You want to start acting as if. It may sound crazy, but you can even speak to your soulmate (although not when other people are around). If you live alone, set an extra plate at the table and have a chat with your soulmate. It's silly, but what do you have to lose by doing this?

It also doesn't hurt to use Feng Shui to improve the energy in your home. There are different styles of Feng Shui, so do a little research and see which one you're drawn to. Apply the tips all around your home. If anything, remove cactuses from the inside the house. They are energy killers. If you have any pictures of yourself alone, or artwork depicting single women around the home, remove them. Replace them with pictures of couples to draw that energy in. You can even hire a reputable Feng Shui consultant to come into your home to help you.

SIXTEEN
What's Your Purpose?

If your soulmate could observe your life right now, would you be proud of what s/he could see?

If you're waiting around for a lover to fill your life and make you happy, you're selling yourself (and your soulmate) short. You must find your purpose, find the things that makes you happy. You're in this world for a reason, and it's not just to be someone's lover. Do you know what your purpose is yet?

If you are already living your passion through your job, great! If not, don't worry. Ideally, it would be great to love your job, but there are other ways to live your passions.

I recommend taking The Passion Test from the book of the same name by Janet Bray Attwood and Chris Attwood. There is a free worksheet based on the authors' work that can get you started. You can find it here:

http://static.oprah.com/pdf/passion-hexagon.pdf

Once you've whittled down your top 5 passions, how can you start exploring your passions? Make a plan to schedule time for the activity, research which classes to take, where you can meet people with similar passions, or book trips (if you need to travel for the activity).

When you're flying high on life, you'll be more attractive because you're happy doing what you love. Who wouldn't be able to resist that?

PART TWO: Letting Your Soul Mate In!

SEVENTEEN
Who's Your Soul Mate?

Okay, you've done some pretty heavy emotional inner work so far. You've released the past, you're looking and feeling your best, your home is welcoming and you've starting to live your passions. Now we can get to the fun part.

Make a list of all the qualities you want in a dream partner.

You can also make a list of non-negotiables. If smoking or not wanting kids is a deal breaker, that goes there. If you want someone with green eyes, that's probably not a non-negotiable if you're also open to someone with blue eyes. Be specific, but also be open. God knows your heart. Ultimately you'll end up with someone who is perfect for you, and some of their endearing traits might even surprise you because you've never even considered them.

Making this list is for you to get clear on what you want and don't want.

If you have a very long list, whittle it down to your top 10 traits. If you have a hard time doing this, use The Passion Test. You might be surprised at which 10 traits are most important to you. Chances are the physical won't be nearly as important as the personality traits and values.

Go further in this work by envisioning the life and lifestyle you want to create together with your soul mate. What can the two of you do together? How do you feel when you are together? Are you affectionate? Do you laugh a lot? Are you open with your feelings? Do you support each other? Do you inspire others with your love? Do you share common morals and goals?

At the end of this entry, write and say aloud, "This or something better now manifests for me."

It's also important to keep in mind to exhibit some of the qualities you want in a soulmate. If honesty is at the top of your list, are you honest and faithful with others in your life? If you're looking for someone in good shape, are you also in good shape? And so on.

EIGHTEEN
Welcoming Your Soul Mate in with Heart Energy

It's amazing, isn't it? There is someone living, breathing and walking around the earth right now who is perfect for you. Welcome this person in with a meditation.

Sit somewhere where you can feel comfortable and grounded. Close your eyes and relax your breathing. Focus on your heart energy. Imagine a golden light emanating from your heart. It becomes a lotus flower of light around you and it shoots out sparks of light into the universe. These sparks reach your soulmate.

As you send out love energy, say aloud, *"I open up to my divine love. God, thank you for my soulmate, who is coming to me right now. I bless him/her wherever s/he is and trust that we are brought together at the perfect time. I release any doubts in my heart or mind that love is mine. I have faith in you God and I thank you for all the love in my life."*

Make it a practice to send out heart energy and meditate every day. Not only will this help you get in touch with the love inside you, heart energy is very powerful and magnetic. Your soulmate will feel it. Meditating also helps still the mind. When you have better control over your mind, you'll have an easier time rejecting the negative thoughts that don't serve you.

Whenever an old fearful thought does show up, choose one of the positive affirmation you came up with to replace the old thought. Break the cycle of negative patterns with conscious effort.

If an old memory still haunts you, sit with it. Let yourself see the memory. See divine light being poured into the memory and watch it drift away.
Tell yourself, *"I will not let (negative memory) re-enter my consciousness. I have cleared the way with positive energy, eradicating the bad feelings, and I have the power to fully let go, to live in the moment. I have changed course."*

Whenever you are feeling low, choose a positive affirmation to say to yourself.

Once a medium shared this affirmation with me. So many people have trouble falling in love because they are not willing to receive love and this affirmation is powerful. Repeat this to yourself 5x, once a day.

"I am now ready to receive love and to be taken care of. I am now ready to give love and take care of somebody else. And I'm willing to bring in someone who's for my highest good and I'm for his/her highest good."

NINETEEN
Raise Your Vibration and Act As If

If you're used to feeling down about being single, this exercise might take some practice, but it's also fun.

So far you've been feeling like a "have-not", feeling sorry for yourself when your coupled up friends are going out on fun dates. When you want something, all you get is the experience of wanting. Start shifting your state from wanting to having. Live as if your soulmate is already in your life. Raise your vibration. Focus on feeling awesome.

When you're walking down the street, pretend you're walking hand in hand with your soul mate. If you're at the park, pretend your soul mate is sitting on the bench next to you, enjoying the afternoon with you.

I had a client do this. She imaged that her soul mate was always to her right: sitting to her right, standing and walking beside her, sleeping to her right. If she was on the subway, she'd leave an empty seat on her right and pretend that he was next to her. Sure enough after a month a man walked into a writing workshop that she attended. He was from out of town and he immediately struck a conversation after class and got her contacts.

If you want to get married, regularly imagine feeling a wedding ring on your finger as you go about the day. Don't know what this would feel like? Get a ring (can be fake) and learn how it feels to wear one on your ring finger.

The more you feel lonely and desperate, the more loneliness and desperation (and other lonely and desperate people) you will attract. Focus on yourself, raise you vibration, expand your heart energy and live as if!

If you don't feel comfortable doing this at first, fake it till you make it. Pretend that you are so happy and in such a loving relationship, living each day as if you're already loved, cherished and appreciated.

Try this for 30 days straight. See how much change comes into your life and write them down. Do you feel more confident? More open and in sync with the universe? Are you being approached more by people (not necessarily potential love interests) who want to talk to you? Do you feel less anxious and more certain?

If you keep happy and act *as if* for at least 30 days, you'll also find the other areas of your life improving as well.

You don't need to tell other people what you are doing. Your ego might try to talk yourself out of doing this, but just give it a try. What do you have to lose by doing this? You're just going about your daily life, and it's fun!

TWENTY
Vision Board

Another fun way to get you focused on the right things is to make a vision board. It's simply a collage of images and quotes of what makes you happy and what you want. When you look at it, it should make you feel positive, and it's a good way of helping you practice the law of attraction.

Buy a poster/bristol board. Cut out inspiring images, words or quotes from magazines. You can also print images out from your computer. Glue the cutouts on your board and place the board in a place in your home where you can look at it often and meditate on it. When guests come over, feel free to hide it. It's personal and you don't need to feel obligated to share it with others.

The vision board trains your brain to focus on the things you want in visual form and it helps you magnetize it into your life.

Don't stop there. Why not use a picture of your dream vacation spot on your desktop? How about a loving picture of a couple on your smartphone background to remind you of the relationship you want?

It's simple and fun to do. And it's amazing what some people have manifested with a vision board.

You can make one specifically for love, or divide the board into four categories: love & relationships, career & money, health & fitness, and spiritual & emotional.

TWENTY-ONE
Expand Your Self-Love

Confidence is attractive. However, don't mistaken confidence for egotism and narcissism. The goal is to love yourself, not to have a bloated ego.

So what does self-love look like?

• Standing up for yourself in a civilized manner.

• Not feeling like you're constantly apologizing.

• Being secure enough to be able to admit mistakes.

• Have no problem telling others if something is unfair, and being able to say no without guilt.

• You're neither egotistical nor self-centred.

• Experiencing minimal jealousy.

• Valuing your own intuition and opinions as highly

as anyone else's.

• Not looking to seek approval from others.

• Having supportive friends.

• Not having money problems & charging what you're worth.

• Able to draw boundaries with others.

• Respected by others at work or in your community.

• Not pretending to be someone you're not.

• Rejection doesn't make you feel less desirable and you understand that it just wasn't the right fit.

• Not letting toxic people into your life and not afraid to create distance with any family members who cut you down.

• Realize that nobody is perfect—you're human and you make mistakes, just like everybody else.

After reading this list, ask yourself if anything sticks out for you. If there is a trait you are not exhibiting, how can you improve on this? Explore in your journal.

Think about three people you really admire. **What makes them great? How can you emulate them?**

TWENTY-TWO
Action vs. Stillness

If you're a type A personality, you're probably itching to go out there, take action, meet people and make this soulmate thing happen for you already. The thing about love is that you can't control the exact day, time and place to meet your soulmate. Filling up your calendar and going to every singles event and blind date that comes your way won't guarantee success if you're doing it with the wrong consciousness.

But this process is also not about sitting back, never going out to socialize, and expecting a soulmate to fall in your lap.

How do you find the right balance? Take a look at what you are doing that isn't working for you.

Do you fall into the first category of treating love like a job, doing everything you can to make it happen that you're exhausted and dejected?

Well, relax. If you've done all the inner work from this book so far, it's time to learn how to generate a degree of stillness inside you so you can listen to your intuition when it offers you clues to the right action. You've already done all you can to welcome in your beloved, and your only job now is to surrender to timing and allow things to unfold organically.

If you're in the second category, where you'd rather spend time in front of the TV than go outside to join the living, make an effort. Go out with your friends, have fun. Doing so will train you to resist your nature of staying at home, where you're avoiding the risk of rejection and meeting new people. The fear of new experiences is controlling your life.

The point is to resist your current nature and to get out of your comfort zone. If you're the type who always waits for other people to approach you, make the effort to sit next to a stranger (doesn't have to be a potential love interest) and strike up a conversation. If you're always forcing yourself to go to every event and talk to every person, hang back once in a while and let others approach you.

Take a genuine interest in other people, and not what they can do for you and your love life. There is always something new and interesting to be learned from other people.

If you genuinely enjoy singles parties, have fun, but some singles events tend to depress people because they can reek of agenda and desperation. Don't go if they make you feel bad. Remember: you can meet your soulmate anywhere, and sometimes in the most unexpected way.

When you're out, don't approach people like they are goals to be accomplished. Don't take it so seriously! Even if you do meet someone who strikes your eye, keep it light. Pressure doesn't help expedite the process. When it's your soulmate, things will happen organically. Be open, be light and have a good time.

Continue living your passions and enjoying only the activities that are fun for you. Carve out time for yourself to meditate and listen to your intuition. Pay attention to synchronistic meetings and follow your intuitive hunches. Stay balanced so when you do act, you're not doing it out of fear and desperation. Change your routine, even a little bit, so you're not always on autopilot going through your day. Be present. Keep positive and happy. Anytime you're having a hard time with this, journal your experiences and feelings.

Manifesting is a balancing act between being and doing. Listen to your gut. Is it telling you to relax? Then take the time to relax and just be. When you're inspired to take action, go all out.

TWENTY-THREE
Putting Your Fears to Rest

Yes, dating can be awkward and nerve-racking, but it can also be enjoyable and a fun challenge. Dating is a time when you're vulnerable and innate fears can come up. You may attract someone who reflects the worst judgments about yourself. See this as an opportunity to grow more confident about who you are. Address the issues within yourself and cut the bad date loose. The world mirrors our insecurities, so as you keep making the effort to move past your fears and blockages, you'll begin to relax and enjoy yourself.

Some people need the experience of dating to work out these kinds of issues. They might've been shy or unpopular growing up, so dating can help them get out of their shell and be more comfortable in their own skin.

Other people might only need to date their soul-mate and realize that they don't want to date anyone else. But at the end of the day, dating is still necessary. You can't find out more about the other person, soulmate or otherwise, without going on a date.

Make a list of what you don't like about dating. What about it gives you dread? Write down your best and worst dating experiences. List the biggest mistakes you've made in dating and leave a few lines of space under each story. When you're done, go back and give yourself advice on how to correct these mistakes. For example, "be more honest", "listen more", "don't take the date so seriously".

The dating experiences you've had were good learning experiences. Moving forward, relax and enjoy yourself. Write and say aloud, "My love comes to me in a way that is fun and easy for the both of us."

If the typical dinner and a movie date is not something you enjoy, it's not the only way to date. Dating is really just getting to know the person. You can do this by having a coffee, taking a walk through the park, enjoying a fun activity together such as wine tasting; you can make it a fun process. What are some things you would like to do on dates? Are there any bars/restaurants/cafes you want to try in your city? If you don't have romantic chemistry with the person, at least you shared a good time and you got to try a new place or experience.

When you're on the date, here are some dating advice to put things into perspective:

• Drop your agenda. Placing too much pressure on one date and one person pollutes the process and dishonors the other person. Make it your goal to simply get to know the other person during the date.

• If you're nervous, engage by asking questions and listening more.

• Know that the other person is human too. S/he might also be nervous, awkward and afraid, so keep this in mind. First dates tend be full of pressure, so it might be difficult for both of you to open up. Don't dismiss the person right off the bat. Give this person a break.

• You don't have to do anything you're not comfortable with. Say "No" if you want to. You're in control.

• Remember that you don't need to change yourself, but you need to be more comfortable with yourself.

• Have rock solid faith that your soulmate is out there and that you can't miss him or her.

• Do you easily find fault in every date? There is no perfect man or woman, only the right person for you. Be aware if your pickiness is a defense mechanism to protect your ego and push others away.

Recognizing these tendencies is the first step. Redirect your thinking and focus on their good qualities.

• You don't need to make the other person fit and you don't need to act like someone else to make your date like you.

Remember to keep it light and have fun!

TWENTY-FOUR
Create a Haven for Your Heart

You're opening yourself up to love and this can be a vulnerable time. Surround yourself with supportive people. You need to protect your heart. You don't need to tell everybody what you're doing. Sometimes well meaning friends and family can play into your worst fears about love and feed your insecurities.

You can train people what not to say around you. **Make a list of people who you need to talk to. Write out what you want them to stop saying to you.** For example, you might have to gently ask your mom to stop mentioning the fertility chances for women over thirty-five if you're past this age and looking to get married and have kids. Or politely ask your best friend to stop telling you how bad dating is in your city. If they refuse to do this, limit your communication with them for the time being.

Now who are the friends you feel supported by?

Spend more time with them. If you don't feel you have enough supportive people around you, as long as you're in this good space, you'll most likely attract new, likeminded friends when you're out doing the activities you enjoy.

Limit what you read or watch on TV if they make you feel bad about being single. Avoid singles events if they make you feel desperate or uncomfortable. Stay strong. Look for great love stories to give you hope. Ask married couples how they met. Love finds people at any age. Notice other happy couples around you and feel good for them. Focus on stories that give you hope. **Write down anything that inspires you. Also journal the difficult moments, because once you have it written down, you should feel a release.**

If you do find yourself writing negative things, go back and write down a positive truth for each. For example, *"I feel I'm always going to be single"* can turn into, *"My single days are coming to an end."*

Stay centered by meditating, praying, reading, doing yoga, taking walks, or whatever you enjoy. Keep your vibration high. Laugh with your friends, make others feel good, do the things you love.

This is a time to stay open. Again, you can't choose how you'll meet your soulmate, so if you are betting on one specific way of meeting them, let it go.

Expect the unexpected.

TWENTY-FIVE
Reject Rejection and Jealousy

If you think of love as a competition, let go of that notion. Maybe you've grown up with the idea that there was not enough love to go around in your family. As an adult, you might look around and wonder why everyone else is paired up and you're left out. You might think that you need to be younger, more beautiful, or have more money to attract love. Drop those lines of thinking if you haven't already.

You're enough just the way you are. Love doesn't have limits. If only gorgeous people got love, supermodels would never get dumped. If only rich people got love, millionaires wouldn't need to hire matchmakers.

If you think only younger people have the pick of the good mates, you're also mistaken. Older people are more secure with themselves and have a better idea of the lifestyle they want to live and the partner they want. One of the reasons the divorce rate is so high is because people marry before they get the time to establish their own identities and know what they want in a partnership.

If you think you need to marry young while you have your youthful looks, what's going to happen when you're middle-aged? A marriage certificate is not going to prevent your partner from leaving or straying if superficial ties were the foundations of your marriage.

If these limiting beliefs just won't go away, journal about it. **What real life examples can you find about people who found love against the odds?** Look at all the celebrities who married after forty. What about stories about people who are deemed "undateable" by others only to find true love? Do you know people in real life who found love against the odds?

There is no competition when you're dating on the soul level. You'll ultimately be with the right person for you. Be happy for others if they are happily in a relationship because it allows the subconscious mind to believe that love is also possible for you. Did you know that the subconscious mind doesn't know the difference between what you feel for yourself and other people?

If there is someone in your life you feel threatened by, someone who always seems to get the guy/girl, bless this person. Write and say aloud: *"I bless (person) for getting his/her love. We both get love, and my love can't see past me."*

Don't be too hard on yourself if you are jealous. Try to understand where the jealousy is coming from. It's a good indicator of what you really want. If you're jealous of your best friend because she has a boyfriend, do you want her boyfriend, or a relationship similar to what they have?

You can choose how to use the feeling of jealousy. You can either become a resentful green-eyed monster, or you can choose to feel inspired. If it's possible for another person to have this, you can also have it.

There is enough love and happiness for everyone. Think in abundance. Comparing yourself to others is silly. Just because your friends are paired up, it doesn't mean you're doomed to be alone forever. Love is not a numbers game. It only takes one. Love can happen suddenly and not only will you catch up, you may even surpass your friends in terms of quality of relationship. You're doing a lot of inner work, and not settling for quick fixes. When you get love, it will be long-term and truly fulfilling for the soul.

If you are dating and the person you're seeing is not

calling you back, don't take it personally. Of course this is easier said than done, especially if you really liked the person. If you're wondering what you did wrong, and what you could've said or done to make the person like you, stop. There's nothing that can keep your real soul mate from you. Have you ever rejected someone who was a lovely person, but you just didn't feel a connection with them? Just because they weren't right for you doesn't mean there's anything wrong with them or that they don't deserve love. They're just not the right fit. Someone else might feel the same about you, so don't take it personally.

Sometimes you might go on several dates with someone promising, or even have a short-lived relationship. If it ends, let it go. Their purpose in your life might've just been to help you open up to your soulmate, especially if you haven't dated in a while. We have the potential to grow in every relationship, so thank them for helping you on this journey.

Repeat this to yourself whenever a date doesn't work out the way you wanted it to: *"They're not the right fit."* Thank this person for not wasting another minute of your time.

While rejection will inevitably give your ego a little bashing, your soul always remains whole, complete, perfect. If you're still upset, journal your thoughts as to why you're feeling that way. Turn it around.

Remind yourself the positive angle of the situation. There's always an optimistic outlook or a good lesson in an experience, even if you don't see it until later down the line. By being positive, you're changing your brain chemistry and your reality.

Don't try to suppress negative emotions however. Feel whatever emotion comes up, and examine it. If you want to cry, cry! Don't fight it. Acknowledge its existence. Ask what it wants to teach you. Chances are, after a few minutes of really feeling this emotion, you'll be tired of it and will want to disassociate from it.

If someone said something to hurt you, tell yourself that this person is revealing an aspect of themselves that has nothing to do with you. A hurtful remark says more about the abuser than the victim. However, it is triggering a pain in you, so it gives you a chance to identify what you fear. Instead of remaining in fear, explore how you can replace the fear with faith. Don't dwell on the pain any longer. You're okay and you're not wasting another moment worrying about this.

If someone continuously disrespects or abuses you, establish a zero tolerance policy for negative behavior. **Make a list of what you won't tolerate from others**. Ex: "I won't be yelled at by others" or "I won't accept being made fun of for my weight."

Tell the person calmly, "Please don't speak to me that way." You might need to gain distance from an abuser. Keep working on it.

By doing all this, you're telling the universe how you want to be treated. Keep journaling whatever negative feelings that come up. Try to see the lesson in the situation and move on. Don't let other people's negativity get a grip on you. You might even want to visualize yourself surrounded by a white bubble of light that protects you from outside harm.

Whenever fear, stress and doubt descend, breathe. Inhale deeply through the nose and exhale through the mouth. It'll calm you down. Repeat a positive mantra. Stay positive.

TWENTY-SIX
Holiday Survival

Ah, the holidays, a time for sharing, caring, exchanging presents and…feeling horrible about your single status?

Don't fret. Once you're with your soulmate, every lonely or awkward New Year's Eve and Valentine's Day will be forgotten; you'll be too busy having fun with your beloved! Don't get embarrassed about being single. Other people are usually too self-absorbed to notice anyway. If they do make any comments, or ask why you're still single, let their comments roll off you. Deep down you know it's only a matter of time before you're with your soul mate. Other people's insensitive comments won't change that. If you need to respond, simply say that you're not too worried and you're enjoying yourself in the present moment.

Keep up the high vibration and live "as if". Buy a

card for your soul mate and write something lovely (and give it to them in the future when you've met them). Send love and heart energy to your soulmate. This person is living and breathing somewhere, and eagerly anticipating your arrival too!

Take good care of yourself. Pamper yourself. Don't succumb to a date with someone you're not interested in simply to have a date. That'll make you feel worse. It's better to be with friends you know you'll have a good time with.

If you're feeling really blue, write in your journal about how you would spend the next holiday, when you're united with your soulmate. What would you do together? Describe your dream holiday and keep the hope and the vibration on high.

At present, still enjoy yourself. Be with friends and family you love. If that's not an option for you, the holidays are about giving back, so do so! Give love to the people around you. Volunteer, and do nice things for others, even anonymously. This is the last holiday you'll be spending single, so make it count.

TWENTY-SEVEN
Soul Mate Bucket List

If you woke up and realized you were married to your soulmate, how would you react? What would you do? How would you spend your day, your weekend?

This exercise is all about continuing to build on the excitement of being with your soulmate. **Make a list of things you want to do with your love once you are together.** You have a lifetime of experiencing different adventures and sharing romantic moments together, so what would you do? Share a kiss on a gondola in Venice? Picnic under the Eiffel Tower? Take a road trip across America? Give each other massages? Go scuba diving? Take tango lessons together?

TWENTY-EIGHT
The Final Secret

When your vibration is high and you're happy, you're naturally more attractive. You might feel that more people are magnetized to you and want to talk to you. But beware not to fall for the first person you meet! Take it slow. Take the time to get to know this person.

If you fall into relationships blindly and too quickly, you're sending the message that you're grasping on to someone to save you. Love is not a race to the altar. Make sure that your relationship is not a superficial one based on only infatuation. Don't rush into the sexual component either. When you have sex with someone, you experience oxytocin, which is a bonding chemical, making you feel more connected with this person than you really are. You get the sense that you have more in common than you really do.

If an ex-boyfriend reappears in your life, begging you to take them back, they might have sensed that you've released them, and that you're now happier and more independent. If they once had you wrapped around their pinkie, they're now afraid of losing control over you and will say what you want to hear to get you back. People want what they can't have. Again, take it slow. Remember why you broke up. If you do believe that this person deserves a second chance, proceed carefully. Listen to your inner voice; trust your inner guide.

Journaling in both cases can help you clarify your feelings.

Don't settle for "faux-mates". You've done a lot of inner and outer work so far. You're looking for your Big Love. S/he is out there! Sometimes you have to wait for the right thing. If you fill the space you've made for your soulmate only to let in mediocre love, you'll deny yourself of what you really deserve. That's why you shouldn't be afraid of taking your time to really get to know the person.

Now I'm going to tell you the secret formula for manifesting what you want:

1) Have the desire.
2) Let it go.

So far you've built your desire and the opening to

receiving your soul mate. Now you must let go of how you're going to meet him or her. That means to stop worrying, to stop fretting about so-called missed opportunities, stop doing things with an agenda, stop feeling impatient and frustrated. Some people tend to give up at a certain point and try to suppress their desires, so they won't be disappointed. Stay optimistic and open. The law of attraction works when you can see yourself with the outcome, while letting go of how to get it. Let the universe guide you. Have certainty.

How will you do this while you're waiting? Again, do the things you love, live a full life, share with others, and not focus so much about the outcome. That is the work that you must do. **The secret is to be happy whether you get the thing you want or not.** Stay grateful—more on that in the next chapter.

TWENTY-NINE
Gratitude and Staying in the Present

While you're waiting patiently, have gratitude. Stay in a positive vibe by being grateful for what you already have. Your life is already full of love. You have a roof over your head, food to eat, clothes to wear, money in your pocket to buy a cup of gourmet coffee. **Write in your journal about all that you're grateful for, big or small:** friends, family, pets, your home, nature, etc.

Trust in timing, the process and your inner guide. You can't miss your soul mate. The universe will keep throwing you in situations together until you get together! Sometimes you won't recognize your soulmate at first, which is why it's good to be open and to really get to know someone. It's not unusual for soulmates to "dislike" each other at first, if one or both are afraid of big love. But when you're ready, you're ready.

Be proud of the work you've done. You don't have to be 100% perfect and ready to have your soul mate. You've done your best, went out of your comfort zone and put in a lot of work to get here.

If you're frustrated because you're waiting and waiting, this is an opportunity to exercise patience. Sometimes we make a god out of human love, and that needs to be broken. While you don't have to abandon the desire for human love, as that is a beautiful thing and our destiny, we belong to God. This higher power alone can fulfill our deepest desires and is the source of our joy. The human heart is made for love and we are always searching. But we can encounter it quickly if we let it find us. If you align yourself with God to pursue the passion and purpose that God is calling you to be, you become more attractive to the person you're seeking.

Patience keeps you from taking the wrong actions out of desperation. When you're impatient, you settle. Live in the Now. By continuing your inner work, releasing past relationships and negative thoughts, boosting your self-esteem, socializing and keeping spirits high, you expedite the process.

You already have a destination in mind, and while keeping that clearly in your mind's eye, you can also enjoy the journey. Appreciate all the people you meet, the learning experiences you have along the way, the exhilarating adventures, the laughter. What about the moments of peace, of a new self-awareness and a self-love emerging?

Remember all the odd ways you've met people in the past and how unpredictable it was. Draw closer to supportive friends and family as you continue to open up to love. Be in the present. Love is all around you. If you wait for Mr. or Mrs. Right to show up before you can shower someone you love, think of all the love within you that's going to waste. How can you express more love to your friends, your family, your coworkers right now? Think about how proud your soul mate would be to witness your life when you tap into the abundance of love.

THIRTY
Higher Purpose

When your soulmate is here, you'll probably want to escape into your own world and enjoy each other's company. While the honeymoon period is a magical time when you get to find out all about each other for the first time, remember that your soul mate relationship, the reason why the two of you are fortunate enough to unite on earth, is for a higher purpose.

Focus less on the happiness you'll extract *from* the relationship and more on the joy and love you want to bring to the relationship. You're here to help each other move closer to Spirit, realize your true potential, and to bring more love into the world.

Constantly ask yourself, "How can I share within my relationship and outside of it?"

When you're too focused on the other person, you

risk losing sight of yourself. Don't be co-dependent, be inter-dependent. That is, you are still two separate people who are working together, side by side, each with your own set of strengths and talents that complement the other.

If you ever feel you're losing sight of yourself in a relationship, remember that your relationship is with first and foremost with God. Whose heart are you trying to please?

The Soul Mate Checklist

The universe is always listening, working in your best interest to bring you what you desire. If you meet people along the way who are the wrong fit, don't worry. Just keep your energy positive.

Go through this checklist to ensure that you've removed all the blockages to love.

• Have you clarified why you want love and what you're looking for in a soul mate?

• Do you believe your soul mate is out there and looking for you too?

• Have you released any negative beliefs and behaviors about love and relationships?

• Have you released any negative beliefs about yourself?

• Have you released ex-lovers to make room for new love in your heart?

• Have you forgiven the people in your life for any past hurt they have caused you?

• Have you forgiven yourself?

• Have you realized your true purpose and living a life of passion?

• Have you realized how great you truly are and how much you have to give in a relationship?

• Have you made your home ready to receive your soul mate?

• Have you made your heart ready to receive your soul mate?

• Have you surrounded yourself with supportive people?

• Have you let go of rejection and taken a lighter, more fun approach to dating?

• Have you become more open to the people around you, and taking an interest in them?

• Have you made it a practice to send out heart energy and meditate every day, tapping into the love within you?

• Have you raised your vibration and acting as if your soul mate is already in your life for **30 Days straight**?

If you find yourself avoiding one or more of these things, examine why. Do you want love more than you're afraid of it? The very thing that you're avoiding might be the thing blocking you from receiving love.

If you have any deep-rooted trauma and pain that you can't release as easily, it's advantageous to find a counselor to help you through it. Get referrals and find someone who is highly recommended. The right counselor can make all the difference.

Hypnotherapy can also help those with deep-rooted beliefs. A few sessions can help you heal and break some negative thought patterns. Again, do your research and find someone reputable.

The Love Book

Conclusion

When you're with your soul mate, you feel as if you've known each other forever. Laughs and conversations flow easily and there's no shortage of sexual chemistry. You share the same morals and values, while being different people with unique interests and complementary personality traits. The universe brought you together to bring out the best in each other, and to support each other's growth.

Sure, there might be some bumpy rides along the way. You're human. Just because you're in love doesn't mean all your problems are behind you. While your soul mate relationship will be enjoyable, there's work on your part to ensure that the relationship is a loving, fruitful and long-lasting one.

Vow to each other to always be supportive of one another. Agree on a zero tolerance policy for bad-mouthing, and tell your friends and family never to say one bad thing about your partner to you. As you keep growing and evolving together, never take this gift from God for granted. Life can get in the way, but set aside time alone, at least once a week, for romantic dates to reconnect.

Don't make this person your source for all your joy and happiness. Allow them to be their own person, and don't control them or get upset when they are not acting the way you want them to. They may be your soul mate, and you undoubtedly share a special connection, but they're not mind readers. Making an effort to communicate will go a long way. Stay in awe of one another. Before you met this person, they only existed in your dreams. Now they're in front of you! Never take this miracle for granted.

Keep journaling throughout your love journey. When you read back on your entries, you'll realize how much you have grown, alone and united, with your One.

—Elizabeth N. Doyd.

About the Author

Elizabeth N. Doyd is the author of the bestselling books *Write Him Off: Journal Prompts to Heal Your Broken Heart in 30 Days*, and *Gratitude Journal: 52 Writing Prompts to Celebrate Your Wonderful Life*. She also works as a relationship expert and spiritual counselor, having studied Kabbalah, Buddhism, hypnotherapy, astrology and Reiki.

Originally from Montana, Elizabeth has traveled around the world and currently lives in The Hague, Netherlands, with her husband, son and two Scottish terriers. Her highly practical self-help books are for those looking for guidance and healing in love, wealth and self-worth, and how to live each day with love, joy and purpose.

Elizabeth N. Doyd

Made in the USA
Columbia, SC
05 May 2021